When Your Husband is a Christian—
But Doesn't Always Act Like One

52 Verses to Lift You Up

Mary Stone

Disclaimer: This book is not intended as a stand-in for counseling or therapy. The verses and subsequent messages are intended to encourage, enlighten, and help you grow individually and relationally in your marriage. The Holy Spirit is the one true Counselor Who seeks to provide you and your spouse guidance and healing.

When Your Husband is a Christian—But Doesn't Always Act Like One

Copyright © 2024 by Mary Stone

Paperback ISBN 979-8-9888863-3-4

eBook ISBN 979-8-9888863-1-0

Front Cover Design by Maida: fiverr.com/design_maida

Interior Design and Formatting: Creavision@rahuljhabak123

Also by Mary Stone

Non-Fiction

Run in the Path of Peace—the Secret of Being Content No Matter What

When Your Wife Gets on Your Nerves—or Worse; 52 Verses to Bolster You

When You Have an Unsaved Loved One; 52 Devotions to Give You Hope

Fiction

In BeTWEEN TROUBLE

Table of Contents

When Your Husband is a Christian—But Doesn't Always Act Like One

52 Verses to Lift You Up

Why 52 verses?

When you focus on one verse throughout the week, and others every week of the year, you store these verses in your mind and heart. By repeating, you go deep within scripture, mining the treasures God has for you in those portions of His Word. In this, you will be encouraged, strengthened, and armed to intercede for your loved one.

Although each of the following verses begins with something your husband does or doesn't do, this book is not about him. It is about *you* and how you can use each situation to grow in Christ. Some circumstances will apply to you, others won't. Those that don't, offer you an opportunity to praise God that your husband doesn't behave in that manner, and the opportunity to lift up in prayer your sisters in Christ who do live in those conditions. However, the more of these 52 instances you encounter, the more occasion you have for spiritual growth.

The scriptures given for each situation are not exclusive but rather interchangeable with other circumstances. So if one week's issue doesn't apply to you, please claim the verse to help you flourish, regardless.

As well, this book is not about how to have a perfect marriage but rather how to thrive within an imperfect marriage. The reality is, not one of us is perfect. We all have our faults. As you move through the messages, ask yourself, "Am *I* guilty of this?" Ask God to shine a light upon your behaviors and thoughts. Herein is more room for growth.

Communication with your spouse is vital. However, another reality is, not everyone is willing to discuss issues. You can only do what you can do—be open and non-critical in your approach to invite your husband to converse.

As a marriage and individual counselor for many years—having the opportunity to work with those from various ages, backgrounds, cultures, and faiths—I encountered the issues you will read in the following 52 weeks of verses. These matters are best addressed between partners who are devoted to Christ. Even then, although both are saved, not everyone responds to making changes in a godly way. It is up to *you* to respond in the way God leads as you entrust your husband to Him, for only the Lord can change any of us.

The pages speak of some behaviors which are sin. However, the majority of these husband behaviors fall short of honoring 1 Peter 3:7, which calls husbands to be considerate, understanding, respectful, and to treat wives with gentleness and tact. That said, the intent of these verses is not to criticize or accuse your spouse but to provide a way for you to not only persevere but to prosper in the circumstances and grow in Christ.

As you move through the verses, I encourage you to utilize . . .

7 Essential Elements

1. Pray for your husband and yourself.

2. Ask God to help you see the situation through His eyes.

3. Ask God for wisdom.

4. Converse with your husband.

5. Accept that you cannot change your spouse—only yourself.

6. Pick your battles.

7. Forgive and continue to forgive.

"I will praise the LORD, who counsels me; even at night my heart instructs me. I keep my eyes always on the LORD. With him at my right hand, I will not be shaken."—Psalms 16:7-8

Week 1   When your husband growls at you before his first cup of morning coffee . . .

"I gain understanding from your precepts; therefore I hate every wrong path."—Psalm 119:104

If it is common for your husband to need space first thing in the morning, and you know this about him, then what is there to do but honor that need? It will cost you nothing in the grand scheme of things—even though you may be one who is bright and chipper as soon as you bound out of bed. Or not.

Either way, there is much to be said for bearing with your husband in love as you follow God's precepts, walking in Christlikeness. God honors your faithfulness to Him and to your husband by spreading His peace throughout your household. In this, your marriage will become more unified and mature.

Toward that end, ask yourself, *How do the differences between me and my spouse help us both grow, not only within ourselves but within our relationship?* This is a question worthy of spending time in contemplation. Perhaps this is a great conversation starter between the two of you . . . after morning coffee.

But before you pose the question to your husband, pray for God to reveal your differences in a way that would circumvent condemnation or criticism.

If your husband doesn't like to be spoken to when he first gets out of bed, how can you make yourself helpful, yet scarce?

Week 1 Reflections

Day 1 This week's verse in full, or a portion thereof:

____

____

____

Day 2 This verse empowers me to:

____

____

____

Day 3 My response to the entreaty at the end of the message:

____

____

____

Day 4 What I most appreciate about my husband this day/week:

____

____

____

Day 5 Prayer:

____

____

____

Week 2   When your husband gets on your nerves . . .

"Catch for us the foxes, the little foxes that ruin the vineyards, our vineyards that are in bloom."—Song of Songs 2:15

This verse is a metaphor for things that niggle their way into a relationship and eventually destroy it. In essence, small issues can spoil the love between you and your husband.

What does your spouse do that gets on your nerves? Is it the way he approaches things? Is it that he doesn't place the same degree of importance on things you consider of utmost concern? Or maybe it's because he takes more time to answer your questions than you think necessary. If it's the way he clears his throat or never closes drawers, or other mannerisms that bug you, then simply ask God to give you a blind eye or a deaf ear to these.

Beyond those minor irritating mannerisms, whatever other little foxes may exist, it merits identifying them—and deserves recognition that you each have your own way of approaching situations and life in general.

The Myers-Briggs Personality Inventory is available for free online through several websites. By taking this test, you may gain insight about yourself and your loved one. While this assessment is not infallible—although it has been proven to be valid and reliable—it is a starting place to better understand yourself and your husband. This instrument, and others like it, can reveal your strengths, weaknesses, and blind-spots.

Perhaps the best outcome of both of you taking this test is that you will reach an appreciation for your differences and honor each other's needs. With this advantage, you can move forward to make changes in yourself to accept and embrace how God wonderfully created your loved one.

Will you take the time to follow through with a personality test, knowing there are no right or wrong answers or results, but rather useful information and insights?

Week 2 Reflections

Day 1   This week's verse in full, or a portion thereof:

____

____

____

Day 2   This verse empowers me to:

____

____

____

Day 3   My response to the entreaty at the end of the message:

____

____

____

Day 4   What I most appreciate about my husband this day/week:

____

____

____

Day 5   Prayer:

____

____

____

Week 3   When your husband watches TV or spends hours on video games instead of doing something with you . . .

". . . Love keeps no record of wrongs."—1 Corinthians 13:5

There is no doubt about it, electronics have invaded homes all over the world. These intruders rob people of quality time together.

What emotions manifest themselves within you at this loss? Sadness? Anger? Frustration? Loneliness? Relief—because you are able to get your chores done without interference? But even then, when you do want your husband to spend time with you, and he prefers these other forms of entertainment over you, where does that leave you? — Keeping a log of how much time your husband spends on football, the internet, etc.? Or does it leave you wondering how your marriage evolved to this state of existence?

Is it possible your husband initially turned to these activities because at some time you were unavailable to him? There is no doubt about how all-consuming and exhausting your household duties and child-raising tasks are. It may seem more essential to take care of these responsibilities first. However, it doesn't leave you with much energy or awake-hours to devote to your husband.

How about setting a date night to discuss all of this? It is vital for you to prepare in advance your part in how things got to this point. On this special date, tell your husband how much you enjoy his presence.

Will you set up that date when you finish reading this?

Week 3 Reflections

Day 1   This week's verse in full, or a portion thereof:

____

____

____

Day 2   This verse empowers me to:

____

____

____

Day 3   My response to the entreaty at the end of the message:

____

____

____

Day 4   What I most appreciate about my husband this day/week:

____

____

____

Day 5   Prayer:

____

____

____

Week 4   When your husband spends more time with his buddies than with you . . .

"You, LORD, keep my lamp burning; my God turns my darkness into light."—Psalm 18:28

Because your desire is for your husband to make you his priority—second to God—do you feel a knife plunge into your heart when your husband chooses friends over you?

You ask yourself why your spouse spends more time with his buddies, but you can't come up with a valid answer even though you've asked him about this—in an undemanding and non-accusatory tone.

If your husband doesn't shed light on the situation, ask the Lord to shine a light on *you* as you ask yourself if you are tearing your husband down or building him up. Are you including him in important decisions? Does he have a voice in the home? Does he feel valued, or does he see you devoting more time to your children, your job, housework, or your own friends? God will help you unearth honest answers to these questions.

Beyond what the Lord would have you do about those issues, cherish the time your husband does spend with you. He will sense your love and appreciation, and who knows (except God), your husband may then devote more time to you. However, if he doesn't, by concentrating on the joy you do get when you are together, you will come out in a more fruitful state of mind.

What do you need Jesus to change within you?

Week 4 Reflections

Day 1   This week's verse in full, or a portion thereof:

____

____

____

Day 2   This verse empowers me to:

____

____

____

Day 3   My response to the entreaty at the end of the message:

____

____

____

Day 4   What I most appreciate about my husband this day/week:

____

____

____

Day 5   Prayer:

____

____

____

Week 5   When your husband refuses to talk with you about his feelings . . .

". . . I call as my heart grows faint; lead me to the rock that is higher than I."—Psalm 61:2

Do you feel shutout, helpless to help your husband? Does your heart break because you know he must be experiencing emotions that are exhausting and devastating him? If only he would open up to you. You want more than anything to be his helpmate. But how can you be if he won't let you in?

When you try asking him questions or tell him you know something is bothering him, perhaps this only makes him withdraw further inwardly. So then it seems as if you are pushing him away—the opposite of what you intended.

Where do you go from here?

The Lord knows why your husband guards his emotions and what is at the core of his feelings. When you seek the Lord in this matter, you rise above it by setting your feet on the rock that is higher than both you and your spouse.

Once you have left your overwhelmed heart in God's hands, ask Him to direct your husband to someone safe and trustworthy with whom he could and would open up.

Then let go of your desire to know what your husband is feeling.

What will you do to trust Jesus to help your husband?

Week 5 Reflections

Day 1   **This week's verse in full, or a portion thereof:**

____

____

____

Day 2   **This verse empowers me to:**

____

____

____

Day 3   **My response to the entreaty at the end of the message:**

____

____

____

Day 4   **What I most appreciate about my husband this day/week:**

____

____

____

Day 5   **Prayer:**

____

____

____

Week 6   When your husband dismisses or discounts your feelings . . .

"Look closely at me, LORD, and test me. Judge my deepest thoughts and emotions." —Psalm 26:2 (ERV)

When you can do so calmly, share with your husband not that he hurt you, but that you feel hurt, sad, etc. Be careful to avoid sounding critical or condemning. Tell him how important it is for you to know that he cares. If he "gets" that you want to nurture respect and compassion in your marriage, build on this foundation.

However, if he then comments, "Quit being so dramatic. It isn't that bad." Or "Get over it.", and continues to dismiss you, then it is up to you to pay attention to what he shows you about himself. Perhaps he is feeling discounted. You can't change him but you can change your response to him. And you can change your feelings in this situation. It takes work, but instead of feeling disregarded, ask God to transform this into a positive emotional state. You can begin by changing your thoughts. Altered thoughts will birth altered feelings.

For example: *I refuse to let my husband's dismissal of my feelings result in me being emotionally wounded. I have a right to my own feelings and to feel good about myself. I choose to regard myself as God sees me.*

What thoughts do you need to change to help you let go of hurt?

Week 6 Reflections

Day 1   This week's verse in full, or a portion thereof:

____

____

____

Day 2   This verse empowers me to:

____

____

____

Day 3   My response to the entreaty at the end of the message:

____

____

____

Day 4   What I most appreciate about my husband this day/week:

____

____

____

Day 5   Prayer:

____

____

____

Week 7   When your husband walks away or ignores you when you are trying to engage him . . .

". . . the LORD hears when I call to him."—Psalm 4:3

It has been said to be dismissed or ignored is harder to bear than to be yelled at.

When your husband walks away, you may feel not only unheard but helpless in getting him to listen to you . . . as if you are not important to him and frozen out of his presence. If you raise your voice, you realize that only serves to escalate your feelings of powerlessness. The louder you yell, the more you feel unheard.

Later as he begins to talk to you, are you tempted to walk away from him? If so, have you noticed the gap widens between you?

To stop this chasm from spreading even further, ask the Lord to reveal what causes your husband to walk away. Examine your own heart, your words, and your behavior toward your husband. Is what you say to him uplifting and caring? If not, ask God to help you with that. Then wait upon your Heavenly Father. Don't walk away from Him. Expect God to answer, to reveal what you have asked of Him.

If your words are sincere, uplifting, and caring, then pray for your husband's receptiveness but more importantly pray for yourself. Ask your Heavenly Father to change you into His likeness.

Perhaps then you will have a greater understanding of your loved one.

How does God's presence help you draw close to Him when you feel helpless and alienated by your husband?

Week 7 Reflections

Day 1   This week's verse in full, or a portion thereof:

____

____

____

Day 2   This verse empowers me to:

____

____

____

Day 3   My response to the entreaty at the end of the message:

____

____

____

Day 4   What I most appreciate about my husband this day/week:

____

____

____

Day 5   Prayer:

____

____

____

Week 8   When your husband leaves and doesn't say where he's going . . .

"Taste and see that the LORD *good; blessed is the one who takes refuge in him."* —Psalm 34:8

Not that your husband is answerable to you, but it is normal to want the courtesy of him offering information of his whereabouts prior to his departure, especially since you always let him know your plans.

If this leaves a sour taste in your mouth the antidote is Psalm 34:8. The verse urges you to taste of the Lord. How do you do that? Psalm 119:103 shows how— *"How sweet are your words to my taste, sweeter than honey to my mouth."*

If you want to replace the crummy taste left by your husband's actions, recite words from the Bible. This redirects your focus to God, His promises, and allows you to take refuge in Him. And you will be blessed in the bargain!

In short, if your spouse leaves without speaking, so can you. Only you don't need to leave the house, but rather depart from the situation spiritually to take refuge in the arms of Christ.

Do the following words taste sweet to you?

"And the peace of God, which transcends all understanding, will guard your hearts and your minds in Christ Jesus."— Philippians 4:7

"Yet I am always with you; you hold me by my right hand."—Psalm 73:23

What other Bible verses sweetly bless you?

Week 8 Reflections

Day 1   This week's verse in full, or a portion thereof:

____

____

____

Day 2   This verse empowers me to:

____

____

____

Day 3   My response to the entreaty at the end of the message:

____

____

____

Day 4   What I most appreciate about my husband this day/week:

____

____

____

Day 5   Prayer:

____

____

____

Week 9 When your husband always insists on his favorite restaurant or other venues over yours . . .

"Wives, submit yourselves to your husbands, as is fitting in the Lord."—Colossians 3:18-19

Ask yourself, "How important is not getting my way—even occasionally?" Where does it fall in the overall theme of things? Of course, there could be a larger issue at stake here—one of control. If that is the case, perhaps seeing a Christian counselor or pastor together is in order if the following doesn't produce the fruit you seek.

Set realistic and healthy boundaries for yourself. Suggest a compromise. Hopefully this doesn't elicit ire in your spouse. But if this is his reaction, it is important to not feed into his anger, and crucial that you don't get upset. Please understand that your husband may initially become anxious in "losing control."

On the other hand, it could be that your husband takes his role as head of the house seriously and wants to save you the trouble of deciding. Regardless, is it worth an argument?

A win-win option is to let go of the desire to even once in a while choose where to dine with your husband and instead go to your favorite restaurant with your friends.

How freeing is it to let go and let your husband have his way?

Week 9 Reflections

Day 1   This week's verse in full, or a portion thereof:

____

____

____

Day 2   This verse empowers me to:

____

____

____

Day 3   My response to the entreaty at the end of the message:

____

____

____

Day 4   What I most appreciate about my husband this day/week:

____

____

____

Day 5   Prayer:

____

____

____

Week 10   When your husband won't admit he is wrong, won't apologize . . .

"To do what is right and just is more acceptable to the LORD *than sacrifice."*—Proverbs 21:3

You know you are right and you can prove it. In fact, even when you bring up undeniable evidence, your husband refuses to admit he is wrong . . . or apologize for having done something unacceptable.

What emotions or thoughts then arise within you? Most likely it is something from the enemy who relishes stirring up trouble, both within a person and between people. You are not immune to these snares if *you* have a need to be right. Perhaps admitting you are wrong is not a problem for you, but being right when you know you are right, snags you up.

However, the real challenge here is not *Who is right*? But rather, *What difference does it make who is right*? Ten years from now what will have proved more important—being right or maintaining a healthy relationship?

Hence, ultimately, to do right is more essential in God's eyes. It is more acceptable to Him than sacrifice. Amos 3:10 aptly expresses God's grief in this: *"My people have forgotten how to do right."* Although He was speaking of those who had turned away from Him to worship other gods, still, the verse encourages us to always do right.

When your husband insists on being right, what "right" thing does the Holy Spirit encourage you to do?

Week 10 Reflections

Day 1   **This week's verse in full, or a portion thereof:**

____

____

____

Day 2   **This verse empowers me to:**

____

____

____

Day 3   **My response to the entreaty at the end of the message:**

____

____

____

Day 4   **What I most appreciate about my husband this day/week:**

____

____

____

Day 5   **Prayer:**

____

____

____

Week 11   When your husband expects you to take care of all household chores as well as yardwork, even though you have a full-time job . . .

"We are troubled on every side, yet not distressed; we are perplexed, but not in despair; persecuted, but not forsaken; cast down, but not destroyed; " —2 Corinthians 4:8-9

Paul wrote this verse to those he knew were constantly overwhelmed by pressures and stressors.

Because your husband expects you to do "everything," does resentment take up residency inside you? Especially when you are fatigued and overwhelmed? What takes root within you when you feel taken advantage of or feel pressured to meet the unrealistic expectations of your spouse? If animosity sets up shop in your head, do you find recurring negative thoughts toward your husband? If so, the enemy is poised to fan into flames hostility, loathing, and more destructive feelings toward your husband.

But he won't be the only one at the end of this negativity. It is primed to destroy you as well. In the end, it is you who fostered your own undoing. And to think . . . you could have prevented this from happening by not opening the door to this in the first place.

Greg Laurie says it well— "When the devil comes knocking at my door, I say, 'Lord, would you mind getting that?'"

The next time your mind tends toward negative thoughts about your husband, refuse to open that door. Let the Lord get it.

Make a list of the things you actually enjoy doing around the house and yard and concentrate on the sense of accomplishment and pleasure they give you.

Week 11 Reflections

Day 1	**This week's verse in full, or a portion thereof:**

____

____

____

Day 2	**This verse empowers me to:**

____

____

____

Day 3	**My response to the entreaty at the end of the message:**

____

____

____

Day 4	**What I most appreciate about my husband this day/week:**

____

____

____

Day 5	**Prayer:**

____

____

____

Week 12   When your husband is a different person with others than with you . . .

"My flesh and my heart may fail, but God is the strength of my heart and my portion forever."—Psalm 73:26

Do others praise your husband, their words ringing hollow from *your* experience with him? Do you hear how lucky you are to be married to such a charming and thoughtful man?

Watching your husband open doors for other women, hug them in church, or wherever, is exceedingly hurtful when you don't receive the same treatment, even at home. Because he shows this affection for others, you know he is capable of it, yet he withholds it from you.

Do you find yourself nursing a grudge? So much so you are tempted to treat him the way he treats you? When you spiral downward emotionally, your marriage is in jeopardy, as is your relationship with the Lord. These feelings will eventually destroy *you* by eating away at your physical, emotional, and spiritual health.

When *you* embrace your husband, and he hugs you back, still, you would like for him to be the initiator. Here is where the enemy prods you to play the victim role.

When the devil tried to trick or lure Jesus, Jesus responded with the Word of God. Arm yourself with this sword of the Spirit so you, too, can defeat the enemy who wants to work through both you and your husband to destroy your marriage.

Memorize Psalm 73:26. Believe the truth of it. Embrace it and repeat it when you feel yourself slipping emotionally, mentally, and spiritually.

Turn your eyes and heart toward Jesus—away from the pull to feel sorry for yourself and away from the temptation to condemn your husband for his actions. For if you harden your heart to the man you married, you too, will be a different person with him than you are with others.

What victim mentality thoughts do you need to stop from taking you down a dark path?

Week 12 Reflections

Day 1   This week's verse in full, or a portion thereof:

____

____

____

Day 2   This verse empowers me to:

____

____

____

Day 3   My response to the entreaty at the end of the message:

____

____

____

Day 4   What I most appreciate about my husband this day/week:

____

____

____

Day 5   Prayer:

____

____

____

Week 13   When your husband does not show you affection, and/or turns away when you try to kiss him . . .

"The LORD *is near to the brokenhearted and saves the crushed in spirit. "*— Psalm 34:18

To give further attention to this issue from the previous week . . .

Not every man is a romantic, and it is possible your husband grew up in a home absent of affection.

God never wants you to feel unloved. It would be great if those around you always showed you love. But this isn't a perfect world.

What is perfect is God's love within you. It is more powerful and embracing than you can demonstrate in your own efforts. Therefore, draw upon that which your Heavenly Father offers so you can pass it on to your husband. Show him affection, even if your attempts are rebuffed. You are sowing seeds in that currently infertile ground. Trust God to water and tend what you plant.

Look for ways your husband does express his love. Is it in the way he maintains your car, or that he takes out the trash without being asked? Does he come straight home after work, or doesn't demand full control of the television remote control? Seek and you will find how he is devoted to you.

Jesus understands what you need. Rest in His loving arms and soak up His love. Ask the Lord to fill this emptiness you feel.

How will you show warmth and caring to your husband regardless of his response to you?

Week 13 Reflections

Day 1 **This week's verse in full, or a portion thereof:**

____

____

____

Day 2 **This verse empowers me to:**

____

____

____

Day 3 **My response to the entreaty at the end of the message:**

____

____

____

Day 4 **What I most appreciate about my husband this day/week:**

____

____

____

Day 5 **Prayer:**

____

____

____

Week 14   When your husband speaks and behaves as if he knows everything . . .

"Give me understanding, so that I may keep your law and obey it with all my heart."—Psalm 119:34

Has your best friend indicated she prefers to avoid your "know-it-all" husband? Have you noticed you and your spouse don't get invited out with your other couple-friends? If so, the exclusion you feel, along with the irritation of living with someone who has all the answers, is tough to manage.

However, when you turn to the Lord for understanding to maintain a loving relationship with the man you promised to have and to hold for better, for worse, for richer, for poorer, in sickness and in health, and to cherish until death do you part . . . you will find God's favor and grace in this situation.

Generally, when someone seems to know everything, it is an ego challenge. Somewhere in his life, your husband may have endured emotional neglect, lack of respect, or comments about worthlessness. If so, he struggles daily—even into adulthood—with internal insecurities. "Knowing it all" is a cover up to help him to save face.

Ask God for an understanding of your beloved—not that this will change his behavior, but at the very least you will be able to extend grace and mercy to him.

Wield the sword of the Spirit to cherish your husband:

". . . LORD; give me understanding according to your word. May my supplication come before you; deliver me according to your promise. "—Psalms 119:169-170

Week 14 Reflections

Day 1   This week's verse in full, or a portion thereof:

____

____

____

Day 2   This verse empowers me to:

____

____

____

Day 3   My response to the entreaty at the end of the message:

____

____

____

Day 4   What I most appreciate about my husband this day/week:

____

____

____

Day 5   Prayer:

____

____

____

45

Week 15   When your husband is loud and talks over you and everyone else . . .

"Be completely humble and gentle; be patient, bearing with one another in love."—Ephesians 4:2

Patience is hard to proffer in a conversation where you aren't given the opportunity to speak. Yet this is the perfect time and place to practice patience—and silence—as you bear with your husband in love. Or is this a situation where the Lord would have you speak up?

God encourages you to ask Him for wisdom (James 1:5). Then, as you receive and assimilate His wisdom, you are assured *". . . the wisdom from above is pure, then peace-loving, considerate, submissive, full of mercy and good fruits, impartial and sincere. Peacemakers who sow in peace reap a harvest of righteousness."*—James 3:17-18

Peacemakers must possess immeasurable patience. As you cultivate this fruit of the Spirit, you till the ground of faith for an even greater crop: *"But the fruit of the Spirit is love, joy, peace, forbearance, kindness, goodness, faithfulness, gentleness, and self-control."*—Galatians 5:22-23

Fruit such as this never tasted so sweet!

The reward is yours as you wait patiently for this fruit and a harvest of righteousness.

How will you cultivate your spiritual soil in order for the Holy Spirit to sow these seeds?

Week 15 Reflections

Day 1   **This week's verse in full, or a portion thereof:**

____

____

____

Day 2   **This verse empowers me to:**

____

____

____

Day 3   **My response to the entreaty at the end of the message:**

____

____

____

Day 4   **What I most appreciate about my husband this day/week:**

____

____

____

Day 5   **Prayer:**

____

____

____

Week 16   When your husband won't attend church with you . . .

". . . Follow me."—John 21:19

When Jesus told Peter to follow Him, Peter pointed to the disciple who Jesus loved and asked, "What about him?" Jesus' reply was "What is that to you?"

In other words, what Jesus does with someone else is His business alone.

Do you find yourself complaining to God about your husband's unwillingness to go to church? Is a judgmental attitude toward your spouse establishing a foothold within you? Are you starting to doubt your husband's commitment to his Christian faith? If your answer is yes to any or all of these, it is evident your focus is misplaced.

Instead, it is time to fix your eyes upon Jesus. As the song goes when you "Turn your eyes upon Jesus and gaze into His wonderful face, things around you grow strangely dim in the light of His glory and grace."

If you aren't familiar with the beauty and truth of this tune, you can find "Turn Your Eyes Upon Jesus" on YouTube. Several artists offer awe-inspiring renditions.

As you draw near to your Lord and Savior, He will bless you with His presence and love. It is here in His arms where you find solace and encouragement to grow in your own faith—to direct your attention to what you need to do to follow Christ.

Will you spend time now listening to "Turn Your Eyes Upon Jesus"?

Week 16 Reflections

Day 1   **This week's verse in full, or a portion thereof:**

____

____

____

Day 2   **This verse empowers me to:**

____

____

____

Day 3   **My response to the entreaty at the end of the message:**

____

____

____

Day 4   **What I most appreciate about my husband this day/week:**

____

____

____

Day 5   **Prayer:**

____

____

____

51

Week 17   When your husband's loyalty lies with his mother instead of with you . . .

"The tongue has the power of life and death, and those who love it will eat its fruit."—Proverbs 18:21

How frustrated you must feel when your husband goes to his mother rather than trusting you with whatever. You are his wife, his partner, and you want to share in his everyday life—not be replaced by someone else.

The temptation here is to criticize your mother-in-law and accuse her of interfering in your lives. Even if that is the truth, slinging words intended to hurt will only cause further separation between you and the one you love.

John Wooden encourages, "Don't let what you cannot do interfere with what you can do." In this case, you cannot lessen the love your husband has for his mother, nor weaken the bond they have with one another. And, as you walk in Christlikeness you wouldn't want to.

But you can strengthen the bond between you and your husband. Just because he has a strong attachment to his mom doesn't mean you can't have an even stronger union between you and him. This isn't a competition between you and your mother-in-law, even if you perceive she sees it as such. Your tongue has the power of life. Use it to build up your loved one—and his mother.

What activities can you do with your husband that involve only the two of you?

Week 17 Reflections

Day 1   This week's verse in full, or a portion thereof:

____

____

____

Day 2   This verse empowers me to:

____

____

____

Day 3   My response to the entreaty at the end of the message:

____

____

____

Day 4   What I most appreciate about my husband this day/week:

____

____

____

Day 5   Prayer:

____

____

____

Week 18   When your husband criticizes what you do around the house . . .

"Truly he [God] is my rock and my salvation; he is my fortress, I will never be shaken."—Psalm 62:2

Feeling demeaned is a crummy state of being.

Stephen Arterburn offers this wisdom: "Don't let your wounds interfere with your mission."

What is your mission within your marriage? Is it to have everything go according to your vision of marital bliss? Is it to have your husband treat you the way you lovingly treat him? Hopefully, criticism toward the man you married doesn't nudge its way into your thoughts.

Perhaps your mission is to love your betrothed the way God loves you—a worthy goal. However, none of us will ever be able to reach that measure of love. Still, you can strive to love your husband as God has designed for you to do.

What does that look like? Does it mean ignoring hurtful comments? Does it propose you are to silently thank God for this opportunity to forgive? Might it suggest calmly calling your spouse's attention to how his comments hurt you? Whatever manner God has for you to handle these situations rests on the fact that God is your defense, and because of this you will not be greatly moved.

How can you stand firmly on this foundation—your rock, your salvation in this part of your marriage?

Week 18 Reflections

Day 1   This week's verse in full, or a portion thereof:

____

____

____

Day 2   This verse empowers me to:

____

____

____

Day 3   My response to the entreaty at the end of the message:

____

____

____

Day 4   What I most appreciate about my husband this day/week:

____

____

____

Day 5   Prayer:

____

____

____

Week 19   When your husband mocks you when you try to converse with him . . .

"You intended to harm me, but God intended it for good to accomplish what is now being done, the saving of many lives."
—Genesis 50:20

Humiliation. Shame. Embarrassment. These are all tools of the enemy (who is not your husband) to chip away at who you are in Christ. When this eventually erodes your faith and your love for your spouse, you may be left feeling forsaken not only by him but by the Lord as well.

Joseph spoke the words of Genesis 50:20 to his brothers who had sold him into slavery. God had a plan for Joseph and He has one for you as well. That plan includes refining you and drawing you nearer to Him.

Even though Joseph was discarded by his brothers, he did not forsake God. Rather, he drew close to the Lord and solidified that relationship amidst awful situations. E.g. Potiphar's wife accused Joseph of rape and his subsequent imprisonment.

It is hard to understand how your husband's mocking can accomplish something good. Yet, nothing is impossible with God. So, as your husband derides you, use this as an opportunity to snuggle up to the One who created you in His image.

Ask Him how you can salvage good from this situation. God is faithful, and will direct you in the way you should go. In the process, you will become stronger and closer to Him—and hopefully closer to your husband.

Will you use this truth of Ephesians 6:12? —*Your battle isn't against a person but is against evil spirits of the unseen world.*

And cling to the promise of the Genesis 50:20 verse above?

Week 19 Reflections

Day 1   This week's verse in full, or a portion thereof:

____

____

____

Day 2   This verse empowers me to:

____

____

____

Day 3   My response to the entreaty at the end of the message:

____

____

____

Day 4   What I most appreciate about my husband this day/week:

____

____

____

Day 5   Prayer:

____

____

____

Week 20   When your husband criticizes your friends . . .

"She [a wife of noble character] is clothed with strength and dignity; she can laugh at the days to come."—Proverbs 31:25

When your husband criticizes your friends, could it be because he sees them using you? Regardless, do you then avoid mentioning them to him? Or never invite friends into your home? Do you find yourself telling them to phone only when your husband isn't around?

Actually, these are all effective, self-preserving choices. They are indeed, ways you can sustain your strength and dignity.

However, if after telling your husband how much his criticism of your friends bothers you, and he continues to do so, you must accept that you can't change him or his behavior. You can only do what you need to do to maintain healthy friend relationships. God created women as relational beings. So hang on dearly to those women who love you, without allowing these friendships to replace a friendship with your husband.

Equally important is for you to avoid criticizing your husband to your friends. For if you do, you are repeating a pattern of a behavior you object to in your spouse. It takes strength and dignity to hold fast to do what is right. By doing so, Jesus will help you laugh at the days to come. Ask Him for this saving grace.

How might God use your words to build up your husband while at the same time honoring the relationships with your friends?

Week 20 Reflections

Day 1   **This week's verse in full, or a portion thereof:**

____

____

____

Day 2   **This verse empowers me to:**

____

____

____

Day 3   **My response to the entreaty at the end of the message:**

____

____

____

Day 4   **What I most appreciate about my husband this day/week:**

____

____

____

Day 5   **Prayer:**

____

____

____

Week 21   When your husband makes disparaging comments about your weight . . .

"You will keep in perfect peace those whose minds are steadfast, because they trust in you."—Isaiah 26:3

Regardless of your weight, your size does not determine who you are or how attractive you are.

Who you are in Christ Jesus is what matters. You can trust Him to know you are:

Chosen—1 Thessalonians 1:4.

Beautiful—Ecclesiastics 3:11.

Enough—2 Corinthians 12:9.

Wonderfully Made—Psalm 139:14.

Victorious—Romans 8:37.

Beloved—Ephesians 5:1.

Child of God—Galatians 3:26.

Forgiven—Psalm 103:12.

"You are very special and unique, No one on earth has your fingerprints. Therefore, that makes you 'thumbbody.'"—Al Brice

Because you are this very special somebody, you are empowered by the Holy Spirit to keep your mind steadfastly on God and embrace the peace of this. Hold fast to the person God created you to be.

What other characteristics of who you are in Christ can you add to this list?

Week 21 Reflections

Day 1   This week's verse in full, or a portion thereof:

____

____

____

Day 2   This verse empowers me to:

____

____

____

Day 3   My response to the entreaty at the end of the message:

____

____

____

Day 4   What I most appreciate about my husband this day/week:

____

____

____

Day 5   Prayer:

____

____

____

Week 22   When your husband insists on his harsh way of disciplining your children . . .

". . . 'Plant the good seeds of righteousness and you will harvest a crop of love.'"—Hosea 10:12 (NLT)

"Become a 'possibilitarian.' No matter how hard things seem to be or actually are, raise your sights and see possibilities—always see them, for they are always there."—Norman Vincent Peale

It may not seem there is the possibility you and your husband will ever agree on the best way to discipline your children, but with God everything is possible. (Matthew 19:26)

Start with taking a look at how you respond while your husband is in the midst of doling out discipline. Do you interfere? Are you critical of your spouse after the fact? If so, do your children hear or see your censure? If this is the case, you are becoming a house divided against itself.

This is a perfect situation to apply the saying, "You gather more flies with honey than with vinegar." Tell your husband how much you appreciate that he takes his role seriously in correcting your children. Ask him how you can help in these situations. Tell him you would be glad to lift some of this burden from him. Ask if there are certain circumstances he would like you to handle.

This approach may help you plant the good seeds of righteousness.

However, if your husband is abusing your children, their safety comes first, and taking action to protect them is imperative.

How can you help your husband discipline in love?

Week 22 Reflections

Day 1   This week's verse in full, or a portion thereof:

____

____

____

Day 2   This verse empowers me to:

____

____

____

Day 3   My response to the entreaty at the end of the message:

____

____

____

Day 4   What I most appreciate about my husband this day/week:

____

____

____

Day 5   Prayer:

____

____

____

67

Week 23   When your husband breaks your confidence . . .

"Love is patient, love is kind; . . . it keeps no record of wrongs; And now these three remain: faith, hope, and love. But the greatest of these is love."—1 Corinthians 13: 4, 5, 13

After sharing personal information with your husband, you learn he has violated your trust. Will you let your trust in him be shattered? That's one direction to go, but not one which will take your marriage down a healthy path.

Hopefully, you will speak with your loved one about how you feel. It is of central importance to tell him you feel let down, rather than state he let you down. Even though this is a subtle difference, it avoids condemning him. It's even more imperative to stay clear of saying you can't trust him anymore. Now you can move on to use this breach to build a stronger bond between the two of you.

If your husband continues to repeat what you tell him in confidence, you will want to reevaluate the types of things you share with him. Not that you will keep secrets, but there are some things a woman needs to guard internally. The Holy Spirit will help you make these distinctions for a stronger marriage and for your personal growth in Christ.

Carve out a time when you and your husband can have alone time, without distractions. Share what is on your heart. Tell him how much you love him and don't want this situation to come between you.

Week 23 Reflections

Day 1   **This week's verse in full, or a portion thereof:**

____

____

____

Day 2   **This verse empowers me to:**

____

____

____

Day 3   **My response to the entreaty at the end of the message:**

____

____

____

Day 4   **What I most appreciate about my husband this day/week:**

____

____

____

Day 5   **Prayer:**

____

____

____

Week 24   When your husband gets angry with you . . .

"When you lie down, you will not be afraid . . . your sleep will be sweet."—Proverbs 3:24

Being in the presence of an angry person can be not only intimidating but frightening. You may feel trapped—as if there is no way out or around his anger. Perhaps no matter which way you turn, regardless of what you say or do, it does nothing to diminish your husband's ire. In fact, if you try to defend yourself, explain things, make amends, or try to leave—even if only momentarily— it may fan into flames his wrath. Even though his rage may have never resulted in physical violence, still you feel paralyzed.

If this is your situation, what do you do?

Take up the shield of faith as your weapon of defense. In biblical times, soldiers soaked their shields of tanned animal hides in water before going into battle. So when the enemy's arrows ablaze with fire struck the shield, the flame was doused. Petition the Lord for your shield of faith to douse your spouse's anger.

When a person experiences anger, the underlying feeling is helplessness over things of which he has no control. Perhaps your husband feels unheard, misunderstood, or unloved. Ask God to help you understand the source of your husband's ire, and ask the Lord to help your spouse to understand this as well.

Will you take up the shield of faith and the sword of the Spirit to rebuke the spirit of anger and of fear in the name of Jesus?

Week 24 Reflections

Day 1   This week's verse in full, or a portion thereof:

____

____

____

Day 2   This verse empowers me to:

____

____

____

Day 3   My response to the entreaty at the end of the message:

____

____

____

Day 4   What I most appreciate about my husband this day/week:

____

____

____

Day 5   Prayer:

____

____

____

Week 25   When your husband punishes you with silence . . .

"Set a guard over my mouth, LORD*; keep watch over the door of my lips."*—Psalm 141:3

Ecclesiastes 3:7 tells us there is a time to be silent and a time to speak.

Proverbs 21:23 says, *"Those who guard their mouths and their tongues keep themselves from calamity."*

There is wisdom in these verses, but when someone punishes you with silence, the air between you frizzles with tension. It is extremely uncomfortable to be in this environment. Yet, you can't make your spouse talk to you. Could it be that he is being silent to guard his mouth lest he say something hurtful?

It is in your best interest to attribute his silence as that rather than as punishment, even if you believe his intention is to make you suffer. What have you got to lose in thinking otherwise? It beats being mired in thoughts that will sink your soul into a pit of pain.

So, how about asking Jesus to bless your husband in his silence? Pray that God would help him use this time of silence to process whatever is hurting him. Beseech the Lord to give you understanding of what is going on within your loved one, and to help you see this situation in a more positive light.

How will you use this silence to pour out your feelings of frustration and hurt to the Lord?

Week 25 Reflections

Day 1   This week's verse in full, or a portion thereof:

____

____

____

Day 2   This verse empowers me to:

____

____

____

Day 3   My response to the entreaty at the end of the message:

____

____

____

Day 4   What I most appreciate about my husband this day/week:

____

____

____

Day 5   Prayer:

____

____

____

Week 26   When your husband doesn't remember your birthday, anniversary, and Valentine's Day, but even when reminded, dismisses them as being unimportant . . .

"Continue your love to those who know you, your righteousness to the upright in heart."—Psalm 36:10

Your husband's sentiment toward these special days doesn't fit into a sin category. Still, thoughts may flit through your head something like: *If he loved me, he would remember. I never forget his birthday. He ought to know by now how important these days are to me.*

Then, do you ever intentionally make sure there are no reminders in view, such as cards from friends or other indications of these events, because you want him to remember on his own? And when he doesn't, do you sink into a funk? Taking it further, do you somehow punish him with silence? These are all paths down which Satan would have you trod.

You can take the high road and buy your own present or make date reservations. In short, pick your battles—and this isn't one worthy of fighting, especially if your husband is otherwise "upright in heart." In other words, is your husband faithful to you and to the Lord?

How can you continue to show your love and righteousness to your husband?

Week 26 Reflections

Day 1   **This week's verse in full, or a portion thereof:**

____

____

____

Day 2   **This verse empowers me to:**

____

____

____

Day 3   **My response to the entreaty at the end of the message:**

____

____

____

Day 4   **What I most appreciate about my husband this   day/week:**

____

____

____

Day 5   **Prayer:**

____

____

____

Week 27   When your husband cuts you off, and/or makes decisions without discussing things with you . . .

". . . And what does the LORD require of you? To act justly and to love mercy and walk humbly with your God." —Micah 6:8

When you are shut down, shut out, do you feel rejected? Devalued? Powerless?

Whatever behaviors you launch into as a result, are an attempt to get your husband to hear and acknowledge you, especially when the outcome affects both of you.

Which of your reactions work to further communication with your husband—or to push him away? Even if you don't mean to sound argumentative, your husband may see you as disputing his wisdom. Does he contend you "always have to have the last word," when in fact you aren't arguing but simply wanting to consider all the facts and options?

While you don't see yourself as being contentious, perhaps your husband senses you don't trust his ability to lead. Which do you place more importance on, having your say or trusting your husband and building him up?

Even if it doesn't change your husband's actions, what does the Lord require of you? Micah 6:8 says it best. *"To act justly and to love mercy and walk humbly with your God."*

How do you act justly?

God's answer—"Grant your husband mercy and walk humbly with Me."

What does this mercy look like to you?

So that you do have a voice in this, what can you say to show your husband this mercy?

Week 27 Reflections

Day 1   This week's verse in full, or a portion thereof:

____

____

____

Day 2   This verse empowers me to:

____

____

____

Day 3   My response to the entreaty at the end of the message:

____

____

____

Day 4   What I most appreciate about my husband this day/week:

____

____

____

Day 5   Prayer:

____

____

____

Week 28   When your husband consistently makes detrimental choices . . .

"If any of you lacks wisdom, you should ask God, who gives generously to all without finding fault, and it will be given to you."—James 1:5

Of course you would love for your husband to take this admonition and direction from this verse to heart. But remember, the verses and messages within these pages are not intended for your husband but rather for and about *you* and how *you* can grow in your faith.

So, how do you deal with this situation when decisions your husband makes often end up being less than favorable? How do you interact with your betrothed before and during his choice-making? If he shuts you out, has it always been this way? Or did he get to this point because of how you give input?

Either way, it is still hurtful to be excluded from this important part of your marriage.

Some men do better by reading rather than hearing. Would you be willing to write notes to this man you love and tuck them in his lunch or briefcase, or on his favorite chair? Your messages could include how much you support him in his decision-making, and how you respect his willingness to take on this role. It can't be easy for him, especially if the outcomes are not what either of you want.

As James states in the above verse, God doles out wisdom generously *without finding fault.*

What wisdom will you ask God for in this situation?

Week 28 Reflections

Day 1   This week's verse in full, or a portion thereof:

____

____

____

Day 2   This verse empowers me to:

____

____

____

Day 3   My response to the entreaty at the end of the message:

____

____

____

Day 4   What I most appreciate about my husband this day/week:

____

____

____

Day 5   Prayer:

____

____

____

Week 29   When your husband disregards your household's needs for a budget . . .

" 'The silver is mine and the gold is mine,' declares LORD *Almighty. "*—Haggai 2:8

It is a vulnerable position to be in when your spouse spends beyond your means. Does it seem as if you are spiraling into a bottomless financial abyss with no way out? Most likely you have already tried to discuss this with your husband but to no avail. And if you have attempted this conversation more than once, are you accused you of not being supportive of his extracurricular activities, or that you are needlessly nagging?

Would your husband be open to attending group workshops on budgeting? Many churches hold this type of help for parishioners. Perhaps if your spouse is encouraged by other Christian men, he would be more willing to take this issue seriously. If he is unwilling to do something like this, there are helpful workbooks on the market on financial planning for peace of mind which might help you proceed, even if on your own.

The reality is, everything you have belongs to the Lord. So, in actuality, your spouse is drawing from the Lord's bank. If you consider the situation in this manner, can you then leave it in God's hands to convict your husband to be financially responsible?

In addition to prayer, what steps will you take to address this matter?

Week 29 Reflections

Day 1   This week's verse in full, or a portion thereof:

____

____

____

Day 2   This verse empowers me to:

____

____

____

Day 3   My response to the entreaty at the end of the message:

____

____

____

Day 4   What I most appreciate about my husband this day/week:

____

____

____

Day 5   Prayer:

____

____

____

Week 30 When your husband belittles the healthy choices you make . . .

"Hear me, you who know what is right, you people who have taken my instruction to heart: Do not fear the reproach of mere mortals or be terrified by their insults."—Isaiah 51:7

Despite knowing you are making healthy choices, it is challenging to stand steadfast amidst criticism.

Gary Chapman says, "People tend to criticize their spouse most loudly in the area where they themselves have the deepest emotional need."

With this in mind, what needs has your husband expressed to you? What emotional needs can *you* identify within him?

If he carries wounds from childhood or previous relationships, you are not responsible for meeting or healing these needs. Even if you tried to do so, you might come against resistance, or at best, recognize your inability to fix things within your husband. You simply must not make his issues your issues. The healthiest choice you can make is to offer what you *can* give.

What does your husband need in *you*?

The short list is . . . a man needs a wife who:

- Is loyal, supportive, and encouraging.
- Respects him.
- Appreciates who he is and what he does.
- Grows in Godly character.

How can you embrace the above bulleted items to help you not dread the reproach of your husband but persevere in your healthy choices?

Week 30 Reflections

Day 1   **This week's verse in full, or a portion thereof:**

____

____

____

Day 2   **This verse empowers me to:**

____

____

____

Day 3   **My response to the entreaty at the end of the message:**

____

____

____

Day 4   **What I most appreciate about my husband this day/week:**

____

____

____

Day 5   **Prayer:**

____

____

____

Week 31   When your husband ridicules your ideas and/or your hobbies . . .

". . . we also glory in our sufferings, because we know that suffering produces perseverance; perseverance, character; and character, hope."—Romans 5:3-4

When your husband berates your ideas or hobbies, does it diminish the pleasure they provide you? Do you give them up to avoid derision? Or do you look past ridicule and not let it stain your ideas or leisure pursuits?

In the Bible passage above, Paul clarifies the advantages of the staying power of faith in the face of anguishes. The benefits Paul points out are not meant for you to find gratification in these hurtful situations, but rather are a summons for you to place your confidence in Jesus.

When you do, He will help you see this fire you are in the midst of is like that of gold being refined. In short, your suffering melts away and emerges into perseverance. As you persevere, your character takes on a sheen reflective of the glory of Christ, which renders you hope. This hope anchors you firmly on a foundation of trust in the Lord, Who can help you take your ideas to new and fruitful heights.

Stand firm in knowing God has you in His hands and is leading you through the refining fire. This alone is worthy of "glorying" in your sufferings.

How does this image of being in God's hands leading you through the fire give you peace and hope that—through prayer and patience—you and your husband can share ideas and enjoy pastimes together?

Week 31 Reflections

Day 1 This week's verse in full, or a portion thereof:

____

____

____

Day 2 This verse empowers me to:

____

____

____

Day 3 My response to the entreaty at the end of the message:

____

____

____

Day 4 What I most appreciate about my husband this day/week:

____

____

____

Day 5 Prayer:

____

____

____

Week 32   When your husband corrects you in front of your children and others . . .

". . . Oh that I had wings of a dove! I would fly away and be at rest. I would flee far away and stay in the desert; I would hurry to my place of shelter, far from the tempest and storm."
—Psalms 55:6-8

When a critical spotlight shines on you, it is easy to wish you were somewhere else.

Criticism can pierce the core of your identity as a godly wife. Instead of getting nurturing and validation from your spouse, do you feel picked apart, leaving you feeling splintered, shattered? Is this dowsing the love you have for your husband? If so, the real danger here is if you begin to harbor resentment toward him.

Making sure resentment doesn't build and take root within you is something *you do* have control over. One way to take this preventative measure is to be proactive rather than reactive. When it is just the two of you, could you tell him your spirit is drowning in this situation? If you haven't done so already, would you feel comfortable letting your husband know—out of the hearing of others—that you can handle correction if done in privacy?

If your efforts aren't fruitful, pray for insight into how to handle your husband's correction. God will help you listen to constructive criticism, and help you forgive your loved one's destructive criticism.

Ask Jesus to help you accept and appreciate your marriage relationship, regardless of your circumstances.

Week 32 Reflections

Day 1   This week's verse in full, or a portion thereof:

____

____

____

Day 2   This verse empowers me to:

____

____

____

Day 3   My response to the entreaty at the end of the message:

____

____

____

Day 4   What I most appreciate about my husband this day/week:

____

____

____

Day 5   Prayer:

____

____

____

Week 33   When your husband is secretive . . .

"Do two walk together unless they have agreed to do so?"
—Amos 3:3

When you married, you joined one with each other. So, now when you see your husband being secretive, it feels as if you are pulled apart, not going in the same direction.

It is important to acknowledge that everyone needs some measure of privacy. Just as you don't tell your husband everything, you must accept that he won't tell you everything. But the difference between simply not sharing and being secretive is vast.

When suspicion, mistrust, and resentment rear their ugly heads within you, you likely feel nothing short of yucky. God does not want you to carry this muck around. He has made provision for you to rid yourself of this. His arms are open wide for you to come to Him and leave your suspicion, mistrust, and resentment on the altar. When you do, He will cleanse you of these impurities. Ask the Lord for a filling up of love.

Then go to your husband in this love and speak with him about feeling shut out. Tell him there is nothing in his life you won't be able to hear and to handle with the Lord's help. Ask him to pray with you over this situation.

If your husband still doesn't reveal what he has been hiding, there is nothing further you can do about it other than continue to pray and trust your husband to God's convictions and leading.

What will you do to walk hand in hand with God in this situation?

Week 33 Reflections

Day 1   This week's verse in full, or a portion thereof:

____

____

____

Day 2   This verse empowers me to:

____

____

____

Day 3   My response to the entreaty at the end of the message:

____

____

____

Day 4   What I most appreciate about my husband this day/week:

____

____

____

Day 5   Prayer:

____

____

____

Week 34   When your husband brings up your past "wrongs" to throw in your face . . .

"If anyone is in Christ, the new creation has come: The old has gone, the new is here!"—2 Corinthians 5:17

Your husband may not forget your past wrongdoing, but take heart . . . in God's eyes you are no longer condemned.

Your husband may not be willing to forget or forgive your past transgressions, but praise God, He has forgiven you and has wiped away your sins, no longer to be remembered. Hallelujah!

Have you forgiven yourself? More importantly, have you accepted God's forgiveness? If your answer is no to either of these questions, it is time to resolve this. For if you continue to beat yourself up over something from yesterday, you haven't yet embraced what it is to love yourself in Christ. 1 Corinthians 13:5 declares that love keeps no record of wrongs. Couple this with Romans 8:1—there isn't any condemnation for you who are in Christ Jesus.

How can you keep your husband from convicting you again and again? You can't. But you can embrace the truth of 2 Corinthians 5:17.

Visualize who you are in Christ. Imbed the image in your mind of yourself washed clean and standing in righteousness before the throne of God, Who loves you and sees only the new you.

Week 34 Reflections

Day 1   This week's verse in full, or a portion thereof:

____

____

____

Day 2   This verse empowers me to:

____

____

____

Day 3   My response to the entreaty at the end of the message:

____

____

____

Day 4   What I most appreciate about my husband this day/week:

____

____

____

Day 5   Prayer:

____

____

____

Week 35   When your husband points out he does everything better than you do . . .

"If God is for us, who can be against us?"—Romans 8:11

Being in a relationship with one who insists on "one upping" you is exhausting, especially when you don't want your relationship to be a competition. Rather than being a team, one of you is operating solo.

When you first met, did you admire your husband's competitive nature? If so, think back to how that characteristic served him well. Make a list of how this attribute now contributes to his successes, outside your home and within it as well. E.g., if he insists he is better at lawn care, vehicle maintenance, bringing home a paycheck, etc., let him know how much you appreciate these acts and his internal drive to get things done well.

Still, when you are on the receiving end of what seems like rivalry, it is time to discuss with your beloved that God appointed him head of the household and you as his helpmate. Mention how the Lord joined you together to be as one. Ask your husband to identify what skills you bring to the marriage, and how he sees these working with his abilities to achieve a unified goal.

Tell your husband how much you want to be a team, and that you want both of you to be more than conquerors in Christ. (Romans 8:37)

Embrace the verse: *If God is for me, no one can be against me. Allow this truth to set you free from feeling competed against.*

Week 35 Reflections

Day 1 **This week's verse in full, or a portion thereof:**

____

____

____

Day 2 **This verse empowers me to:**

____

____

____

Day 3 **My response to the entreaty at the end of the message:**

____

____

____

Day 4 **What I most appreciate about my husband this day/week:**

____

____

____

Day 5 **Prayer:**

____

____

____

Week 36   When your husband looks you up and down with a disapproving eye . . .

"For we are God's masterpiece. He has created us anew in Christ Jesus, so we can do the good things he planned for us long ago."—Ephesians 2:10 (NLT)

Wow! God's masterpiece, no less. You are a work of art, created by His divine purpose to join Him in doing good things according to the unique abilities and gifts He gave you.

Another of God's masterpieces is the eagle. Neil Eskelin extends this wisdom: "Take your cue from the mighty eagle. At the first sign of a storm, he spreads his wings and climbs above the tempest. The stronger the wind the higher he soars."

You, too, can soar high, right into the arms of Christ, who adores you. You are the apple of His eye! In Zechariah 2:8, God declares the absolute truth of this when He says that whoever touches you, touches the apple of His eye.

Therefore, can you imagine what the Lord sees when he looks upon you? Dwell on this image. Soak it in. Implant it in your mind.

So, the next time your husband looks upon you disapprovingly, lift your head and soar above the censorship and harsh judgment. Fly into the eyes of the One who looks upon you with love, adoration, and delight.

Because you are a masterpiece, what master work will you create today within yourself and within your marriage?

Week 36 Reflections

Day 1   This week's verse in full, or a portion thereof:

____

____

____

Day 2   This verse empowers me to:

____

____

____

Day 3   My response to the entreaty at the end of the message:

____

____

____

Day 4   What I most appreciate about my husband this day/week:

____

____

____

Day 5   Prayer:

____

____

____

Week 37   When your husband displays jealousy when you interact with other men . . .

"The LORD will fight for you; you need only to be still."
—Exodus 14:14

Does it frighten you when your husband shows jealousy while you innocently speak to other men? Do you feel confused because you don't understand your husband's reaction? If so, this gives testimony to James 3:16— *"For where envying and strife is, there is confusion and every evil work."* (KJV)

Subsequently, do you try to defend yourself but to no avail? In fact, does this stir things up even more? Then do you find yourself being careful to avoid men altogether? But that doesn't always work because when your spouse's friends come over, your husband even gets jealous of them? You are in a no-win situation, even though you have done nothing wrong.

What can you do?

Unpack the verses prior to James 3:16. *"But if you harbor bitter envy and selfish ambition in your hearts, do not boast about it or deny the truth. Such 'wisdom' does not come down from heaven but is earthly, unspiritual, demonic."* (NIV vs. 14-15)

There are many kinds of demonic spirits. Jealousy is one of them. Be still in the Lord and silently, yet boldly, claim authority over it: *Spirit of jealousy, I rebuke you in the name of Jesus. By His authority I command you to leave this household and this marriage.*

Repeat this as many times as the situation(s) require(s). How much freer you both will be!

Will you ask your husband to join you in this endeavor to overcome the enemy?

Week 37 Reflections

Day 1   **This week's verse in full, or a portion thereof:**

____

____

____

Day 2   **This verse empowers me to:**

____

____

____

Day 3   **My response to the entreaty at the end of the message:**

____

____

____

Day 4   **What I most appreciate about my husband this day/week:**

____

____

____

Day 5   **Prayer:**

____

____

____

Week 38   When your husband falsely accuses you . . .

"Vindicate me, LORD my God; do not let them gloat over me."
—Psalm 35:24

King David, Jeremiah, and Jesus were all falsely accused, as was Paul.

Oft times others blame us for something of which they themselves are guilty. This is projection—a psychological defense mechanism. That said, this may not be the reason your husband holds you responsible for something you haven't done. Perhaps he truly believes you are guilty because he doesn't have all the facts. Regardless, communication is the key to clearing up this misjudgment.

Avoid using the word "why" since that generally puts a person on the defensive. A question such as, "What is there that leads you to believe I did that?" is softer (if your tone of voice is gentle) and more likely to open the door to understanding.

However, if these accusations are a pattern in your marriage, much more is at stake. Would you both be willing to go to marriage counseling or meet with your pastor? If so, in these sessions, it is vital to avoid "telling" on each other, as if you want to prove your point to a third party.

Rather, approach each other with, "It is important to me for you to believe me." Or . . . "for us to trust each other"; or whatever is in your heart, as long as you are not accusing your spouse of something.

What words will you use to be gentle and loving in this conflict?

Week 38 Reflections

Day 1   **This week's verse in full, or a portion thereof:**

____

____

____

Day 2   **This verse empowers me to:**

____

____

____

Day 3   **My response to the entreaty at the end of the message:**

____

____

____

Day 4   **What I most appreciate about my husband this day/week:**

____

____

____

Day 5   **Prayer:**

____

____

____

Week 39   When your husband lies to you . . .

"Do not take revenge, my dear friends, but leave room for God's wrath, for it is written: 'It is mine to avenge; I will repay,' says the Lord."—Romans 12:19

Do you feel betrayed when your husband lies to you? As a result, are you tempted to be less than honest with him about things?

At some point, all of us are victims of lies. If your husband has lied to protect your feelings, or to avoid conflict, the result is the same—loss of trust in what he says.

Tell him you are more open to the truth than to avoidance of the truth—that you can handle honesty, even if it is hurtful to hear.

However, if you suspect the lie is maliciously intended or is to hide something, you have the choice to forgive (which doesn't mean you condone the lie) and ask God to help you avoid being sucked into the deception. Pray for God's provision to keep you from dwelling on the lie, for holding a grudge and/or getting revenge will corrode your relationship and your own well-being.

Ask God to reveal if your husband has lied as a result of your criticism. Not that this makes you responsible for your husband's behavior, but at least it will help you make a change in your actions and attitude. The goal here is your growth in Christ. You, your husband, and your marriage will all benefit.

How will you embrace the promise of Proverbs 19:11—"A person's wisdom yields patience; it is to one's glory to overlook an offense."?

Week 39 Reflections

Day 1   This week's verse in full, or a portion thereof:

____

____

____

Day 2   This verse empowers me to:

____

____

____

Day 3   My response to the entreaty at the end of the message:

____

____

____

Day 4   What I most appreciate about my husband this day/week:

____

____

____

Day 5   Prayer:

____

____

____

Week 40   When your husband says hurtful things to you and/or calls you names . . .

"You make known to me the path of life; in your presence there is fullness of joy; at your right hand are pleasures forevermore."—
Psalm 16:11

When your husband utters cutting remarks, it is vital that you not let them wound you or cause you to stumble off the path of righteousness. God's path of life is devoid of anything which would get in your "way," but rather is paved with peace and His presence where there is fullness of joy.

When spiteful words are flung at you, duck and put your hand in God's "right" hand where pleasures indeed abound. This will help you stay the course, enabling you to run in the path of righteousness.

It isn't known for certain who penned the following verses from Psalm 119, but it was obviously one who suffered under others' taunts:

"My soul is weary with sorrow; strengthen me according to your word," (v. 28); *"I run in the path of your commands, for you have broadened my understanding* [set my heart free].*"v. 32); "Direct me in the path of your commands, for there I find delight."* (v. 35); *"May your unfailing love come to me,* LORD, *. . . then I can answer anyone who taunts me, for I trust in your word."* (vs. 41-42).

Which verses of God's Word will you hide in your heart to help you run in the path of peace and not be hindered by hurtful words?

Week 40 Reflections

Day 1   **This week's verse in full, or a portion thereof:**

____

____

____

Day 2   **This verse empowers me to:**

____

____

____

Day 3   **My response to the entreaty at the end of the message:**

____

____

____

Day 4   **What I most appreciate about my husband this day/week:**

____

____

____

Day 5   **Prayer:**

____

____

____

Week 41   When your husband uses foul language . . .

"Turn away from evil and do good; seek peace and pursue it."
—Psalm 34:14

To be sure, foul language is evil. God provides four steps to take in this situation:

- Turn away from it.
- Do good.
- Seek peace.
- Pursue peace.

The first action is fairly easy. When your husband uses words that assault your ears, simply turn away. That said, you need to let him know in advance this is what you will do whenever he uses foul language. You must convey you are not turning your back on him, only the words you don't want to hear.

Do good is your next step. Lifting your spouse to the Lord for help in this area qualifies in this category.

Seek peace. This calls for you to avoid arguments over your husband's choice of words.

Pursue peace. Pursuing peace requires you to not let foul language disturb the peace you otherwise have in your home.

When you follow these footsteps God clearly lays out, you will be able to run in the path of peace, for He will have set your heart free from the weapon the enemy had intended to destroy your home.

Make a list of things that give you peace. Escape to them in times of disorder.

Week 41 Reflections

Day 1 This week's verse in full, or a portion thereof:

____

____

____

Day 2 This verse empowers me to:

____

____

____

Day 3 My response to the entreaty at the end of the message:

____

____

____

Day 4 What I most appreciate about my husband this day/week:

____

____

____

Day 5 Prayer:

____

____

____

Week 42   When your husband refuses to tell you he loves you, yet doesn't actually say he doesn't love you anymore . . .

"But you, O LORD, are a shield around me, my glory, the One who lifts my head high."—Psalm 3:3

Every wife needs to know she is loved and to feel loved, of that there is no doubt.

The good news is what Josh McDowell proclaims . . . "The One who knows you best loves you most!"

Is this enough to fill you up? On a spiritual level, yes. On an earthly plain, no. So, what do you do to avoid sinking into a black hole? Do you ask your husband if he does or doesn't love you anymore—probably not the best route to pursue, because what if you don't get the answer you want? If he refuses to discuss this, seek the Lord's wisdom in this heart-wrenching situation. Ask God to show you what He sees in your husband's heart. Then concentrate on what your spouse does do that demonstrates his love for you.

If you put all your energy into wanting to hear the words your husband can't or won't say, you will deplete your "emotional bucket." When you concentrate on what you don't have, you will spiral downward. As this happens, you sink into a pit of gloom and hopelessness. Even worse, you draw away from your husband, and away from the Lord.

How will you embrace sincere love for your husband and the Lord in tenacious love?

Week 42 Reflections

Day 1   **This week's verse in full, or a portion thereof:**

____

____

____

Day 2   **This verse empowers me to:**

____

____

____

Day 3   **My response to the entreaty at the end of the message:**

____

____

____

Day 4   **What I most appreciate about my husband this day/week:**

____

____

____

Day 5   **Prayer:**

____

____

____

Week 43   When your husband tells you he no longer loves you and files for divorce . . .

". . . For we know how dearly God loves us, because he has given us the Holy Spirit to fill our hearts with his love."
—Romans 5:5 (NLT)

How devastated and crushed you must feel when you hear the words, "I don't love you." Do your thoughts fly to things you could have done differently, to what you should have done? Does your mind grope for ways to restore your husband's love for you? Do you emotionally scramble for ways to change all of this, to regain what was in the beginning that is now lost?

Yet, when the dust settles, you realize all this is not within your control. You cannot change your husband. It is worth repeating what has been said previously . . . you can only change yourself and your response to him and this situation.

Kneel before the Lord, your shattered heart in your hands, and present yourself to the One who loves you most. Entrust your brokenness to Him.

God's heart is tender; He loves to create something new and wonderful with the splintered pieces you place before Him. It may not seem possible you will ever feel whole or loved again. But with God all things are possible.

Claim the promise in Jeremiah 29:11— *"'For I know the plans I have for you,' declares the* LORD, *'plans to prosper you and not to harm you, plans to give you hope and a future.'"*

Would you be willing to join a Christian support group for women going through divorce?

Week 43 Reflections

Day 1   This week's verse in full, or a portion thereof:

____

____

____

Day 2   This verse empowers me to:

____

____

____

Day 3   My response to the entreaty at the end of the message:

____

____

____

Day 4   What I most appreciate about my husband this day/week:

____

____

____

Day 5   Prayer:

____

____

____

Week 44   When your husband drinks too much . . .

"The end of all things is near. Therefore be alert and of sober mind so that you may pray. Above all, love each other deeply, because love covers over a multitude of sins." —1 Peter 4:7-8

When people consume alcohol, they can become mean, withdrawn, depressed, and/or talkative—saying things that may or may not be true. On the other hand, someone who drinks in excess may be exceedingly loving. Regardless of which state your husband evolves into, it is key that you don't accept responsibility for, or get hooked into his behavior. Still, no matter which direction his drinking takes, his use and abuse of alcohol affects your relationship.

Does it seem as if your husband chooses the bottle over you? That he anesthetizes himself and what he is dealing with instead of turning to you—or more importantly to God?

Turning to God is a life-saver for *you* in this situation. Take up the sword of the Spirit. Claim God's promises, especially the one in 1 Peter 4:7 — the end of all things is near — and believe God for the end of your husband's drinking. Your husband may not be sober, but you are. So pray and love your husband deeply. God's love for him and for you indeed covers over a multitude of sins.

You have prayed for the Lord to deliver your husband from his addiction, and likely have asked God to heal whatever triggers or entices your loved one to drink. Now, take care of yourself. If you haven't already, join a prayer group comprised of those who have similar requests. Connect with Al-Anon, etc.

What steps will you take to take care of yourself in these circumstances?

Week 44 Reflections

Day 1   **This week's verse in full, or a portion thereof:**

____

____

____

Day 2   **This verse empowers me to:**

____

____

____

Day 3   **My response to the entreaty at the end of the message:**

____

____

____

Day 4   **What I most appreciate about my husband this day/week:**

____

____

____

Day 5   **Prayer:**

____

____

____

Week 45   When your husband gambles . . .

"Ah, Sovereign LORD, you have made the heavens and the earth by your great power and outstretched arm. Nothing is too hard for you." —Jeremiah 32:17

You know gambling is an addiction and you fear for your husband's ruin. As well, you may reach the point of feeling helpless and afraid of losing your home, your sanity, and more. Yet, you feel helpless to intervene. Or, are you without help?

God has promised nothing is too difficult for Him. While you trust the Lord with this troubling situation, embrace Psalm 34:14: *"Turn from evil and do good; seek peace and pursue it."* In your doing good, seeking and pursuing peace, you will be the victor—regardless of your husband's activities.

Even if your husband's gambling drains your bank account, your peace is not dependent upon financial ruin. Not according to God's Word and His promises, anyway.

Still, it would be wise to seek counsel through the church and/or an attorney to find out how you can protect yourself economically. As well, you can get involved with Gam-Anon, a self-help group for those affected by a loved one's gambling. Both you and your husband need help.

What steps can you take, and what good deeds can you do in the midst of your husband's gambling to help you pursue the peace Jesus promises?

Week 45 Reflections

Day 1	**This week's verse in full, or a portion thereof:**

____

____

____

Day 2	**This verse empowers me to:**

____

____

____

Day 3	**My response to the entreaty at the end of the message:**

____

____

____

Day 4	**What I most appreciate about my husband this day/week:**

____

____

____

Day 5	**Prayer:**

____

____

____

Week 46   When your husband has a lingering eye toward other women . . .

"Have mercy on me, LORD, for I am faint; heal me, LORD, for my bones are in agony. My soul is in deep anguish. How long, LORD, how long?"—Psalms 6:2-3

When your husband's gaze strays to other women, it is important to sort out what exactly is happening. Is your husband "looking" because he appreciates beauty, or is he "looking" to go beyond the glance with ungodly thoughts or actions?

If the former, join him in his admiration of God's creation. By making comments such as these aloud: "She certainly is beautiful." "What a great shape she has." etc., will unite you with your husband and prevent jealousy from taking root in you.

However, if you suspect your husband desires other women, then go directly to God for clarification on this. If the Lord confirms your suspicions, your next step is to lift your husband to Him, praying for your spouse to be delivered from this sin. And it is important for you to know your husband's roving eye has nothing to do with you. In days of yore, many believed if only the wife "took better care of herself" then her husband wouldn't search out other women. This perpetuated the belief that a woman "drove her husband to sin."

Hopefully, you haven't bought into this lie, because in truth, no one is responsible for another's behaviors.

What does the Lord reveal for you to do in this situation?

Week 46 Reflections

Day 1   This week's verse in full, or a portion thereof:

____

____

____

Day 2   This verse empowers me to:

____

____

____

Day 3   My response to the entreaty at the end of the message:

____

____

____

Day 4   What I most appreciate about my husband this day/week:

____

____

____

Day 5   Prayer:

____

____

____

Week 47   When your husband commits adultery . . .

"I will instruct you and teach you in the way you should go; I will counsel you with my loving eye on you."—Psalm 32:8

Last week's message dealt with your husband's lingering eye. Jesus clearly addressed this by saying anyone who looks on a woman lustfully already commits adultery with her in his heart. (Matthew 5:28) Perhaps you are able to live with this if your husband is otherwise faithful to you in his fleshly behavior. Or at least endure it while in ardent prayer for your spouse.

However, if you know for certain—beyond a reasonable doubt—that your husband is in the midst of the unfaithful act of adultery, (which is what God calls it instead of an "affair"), you have a decision to make. To help you sort things out, you will want to search the Bible regarding conditions for divorce due to sexual immorality and/or conditions for a wife and husband to separate. Arm yourself by going deep into God's Word. Embrace the promise of Psalm 32:8—*"I will instruct you and teach you in the way you should go; I will counsel you with my loving eye on you."*

You can count on God's faithfulness to you! Yea and Amen!

Do you have an army of trustworthy spiritual prayer warriors to come alongside you in this situation?

Week 47 Reflections

Day 1   This week's verse in full, or a portion thereof:

____

____

____

Day 2   This verse empowers me to:

____

____

____

Day 3   My response to the entreaty at the end of the message:

____

____

____

Day 4   What I most appreciate about my husband this day/week:

____

____

____

Day 5   Prayer:

____

____

____

Week 48 When your husband puts you on a strict allowance . . .

"And my God will supply every need of yours according to his riches in glory in Christ Jesus."—Philippians 4:19 (ESV)

If your husband gives you only what he thinks you need for household items, including groceries, and asks for an accounting after purchases, do you feel like a child who can't be trusted with money? Especially if you have never spent irresponsibly? Do you long to buy something for yourself, such as a latte with your friends, or something more lavish like a pedicure? Are you embarrassed when your best friend asks you to lunch when you know you can't pay for yours, so you make excuses?

You look around the church and see other wives wearing new clothes or watch as they bring yummy meals to potlucks—dishes you know your budget won't allow.

Do you find yourself frustrated and resentful being so dependent upon your husband? Satan relishes it when you go beyond resentment to bitterness and eventually hatred.

God loves it when you turn your eyes away from your circumstances to refocus your dependence upon Him. He promises to supply *all* your needs according to His riches in Jesus. Those riches are infinite, coming from a generous God.

So, as you shift your attention to your Heavenly Father and His promises, thank Him for His provisions. Wait expectantly for these blessings. It is exciting to see what He will afford you. Will the Lord answer your prayers for your husband to freely share your family's income? Will God provide a source of extra income for you to do with as you wish? The Lord Almighty abounds in creative solutions!

Will you thank God for what He has provided, what He is providing, and what He has yet to give you?

Week 48 Reflections

Day 1 **This week's verse in full, or a portion thereof:**

____

____

____

Day 2 **This verse empowers me to:**

____

____

____

Day 3 **My response to the entreaty at the end of the message:**

____

____

____

Day 4 **What I most appreciate about my husband this day/week:**

____

____

____

Day 5 **Prayer:**

____

____

____

145

Week 49   When your husband monitors everything you do . . .

"For God is pleased with you when you do what you know is right and patiently endure unfair treatment."—1 Peter 2:19 (NLT)

If your husband demands to know where you are at all times and monitors what you do, it can trigger a tornado of emotions within you—self-consciousness, nervousness, anxiety, worry, anger, resentment, or fear. Do you then monitor your own behaviors, hoping to avoid offending or displeasing the man you married?

None of this is healthy.

Gently calling out this "being watched" behavior is honest and can be beneficial. How your husband receives you expressing your discomfort when he watches what you do or where you go will determine whether the result is beneficial for both of you.

That said, if this monitoring behavior leaves you feeling controlled and hypervigilant, and you have begun to change who you are to make sure you don't upset your husband, you have crossed over into territory that feels scary and unsafe. This can be an indicator of an abusive relationship. Are situations escalating to the point where you constantly feel fearful of saying or doing the wrong thing?

You want to be the wife with whom God is pleased, while at the same time you know this is not what the Lord considers a loving relationship. The "unfair" treatment spoken of in 1 Peter 2:19 is not the same as "abusive" treatment. Seek the Holy Spirit's guidance as to what to do to be safe and to do what is right in God's sight.

How will you pray?

Week 49 Reflections

Day 1   This week's verse in full, or a portion thereof:

____

____

____

Day 2   This verse empowers me to:

____

____

____

Day 3   My response to the entreaty at the end of the message:

____

____

____

Day 4   What I most appreciate about my husband this day/week:

____

____

____

Day 5   Prayer:

____

____

____

Week 50   When your husband isolates you from family and friends . . .

"And let us consider how we may spur one another on toward love and good deeds, not giving up meeting together, as some are in the habit of doing, but encouraging one another—and all the more as you see the Day approaching."—Hebrews 10:24-25

Before you married, you most likely had a close relationship with family and friends, but now you find yourself cut off from them because your husband either doesn't like them, insists they are a bad influence on you, or he tries to convince you he loves you so much that he wants you all to himself. Even though you and your husband attend church, is he always at your elbow, ushering you away from conversations longer than a few words? At first you found his attention and devotion flattering and you, too, wanted to spend as much time with him as possible.

But now, you miss the bond you had with your parents, your sister, your best friend. You long for the camaraderie and deep— or meaningless yet fun—conversations you shared. You yearn for their encouragement and acceptance of who you are. You miss the laughter, the love, and the lubricant that made your day that much better.

In short, your life lacks the essence of Hebrews 10:24-25. In this desert spot, you are drying up emotionally and spiritually, even though you spend time in the Bible and in prayer— communicating intimately your heart's desire to your Heavenly

Father. God created you to be relational, to enjoy the fellowship of others. He will provide a way for you to reconnect with your loved ones.

Ask God to make this provision for you, and for Him to keep you safe in this process.

Week 50 Reflections

Day 1 **This week's verse in full, or a portion thereof:**

____

____

____

Day 2 **This verse empowers me to:**

____

____

____

Day 3 **My response to the entreaty at the end of the message:**

____

____

____

Day 4 **What I most appreciate about my husband this day/week:**

____

____

____

Day 5 **Prayer:**

____

____

____

Week 51   When your husband cites scripture to shame/control you . . .

"Therefore, there is now no condemnation for those who are in Christ Jesus, because through Christ Jesus the law of the Spirit who gives life has set you free from the law of sin and death."
—Romans 8:1-2

God's Word is a treasure. A treasure to be mined for guidance, encouragement, insight, and how to live freely and joyously within the Lord's will. When Bible verses are used as a weapon—not to fight the enemy—but to be wielded against you, to shame you into behaving according to the inflictor's will, it breaks your Heavenly Father's heart—and yours.

You realize that verbally defending yourself against the one who wants to silence or shame you is fruitless. Fruitless because you cannot prove otherwise to someone who seeks to control you.

How do you guard your heart against this onslaught? Arm yourself with the very Word used against you—the sword of the Spirit mentioned in Ephesians 6:17. Dive deep into the Bible; embrace verse after verse.

In mining God's Word for the truth, you will see that your loving Heavenly Father desires to mend and nourish your crushed soul and spirit.

Fall into God's loving arms. Ask Him to help you discern who you are in Him. Fix your gaze upon His adoring eyes, for then you will see that because you are His child there is no condemnation or shame.

Seek out wise counsel but be careful to share your plight only with those who align themselves with the truth of God's Word. For there are those who may align themselves with your husband's convincing charm that you are to blame. If this happens, shaming only intensifies.

If you are wary of going to anyone local for counseling, you can find help on the internet. One resource is

https://focusonthefamily.com

Another resource which may prove insightful is Darby Strickland's book based on biblical standards, *Is It Abuse?*

Search until you find the resource that best fits your situation. In addition to this, wield the sword of the Spirit to pray for your husband to be set free in Christ—free from lies he believes. Pray that he will not suffer the consequence of shame as stated in Psalm 25:3— *"No one who hopes in you will ever be put to shame, but shame will come on those who are treacherous without cause."*

Cling to the promises of: Psalm 71:1; Isaiah 61:7; Romans 10:11; and 1 Peter 2:6.

Week 51 Reflections

Day 1   **This week's verse in full, or a portion thereof:**

____

____

____

Day 2   **This verse empowers me to:**

____

____

____

Day 3   **My response to the entreaty at the end of the message:**

____

____

____

Day 4   **What I most appreciate about my husband this day/week:**

____

____

____

Day 5   **Prayer:**

____

____

____

Week 52   When your husband physically abuses you . . .

"He will rescue them from oppression and violence, for precious is their blood in his sight."— Psalm 72:14

You love your husband . . . just not the way he treats you. But, you say in defense of him, "Most of the time he is good to me. He doesn't always hurt me. And afterwards he always apologizes and promises to never do it again. Besides," you argue, "no one else could love me. I have nowhere else to go." Perhaps you hide your bruises because you are embarrassed, and/or don't want others to judge you. You fear your pastor and other Christians will insist you stay in this relationship. So you endure and "turn the other cheek." Isn't that what the Bible says to do?

God's Word also says *you are too precious to endure oppression and violence*. It also states, *"If it is possible, as far as it depends on you, live at peace with everyone."*—Romans 12:18. The truth of the matter is, no matter what *you* do to live at peace with your spouse, it doesn't stop the violence. So it is *not possible* to safely live in your home.

Safety is an absolute must!

Pray! Call the National Domestic Violence Hotline: 1-800-799-7233

This hotline is open 24/7 in English and Spanish, plus 200 more languages through interpretation service.

Do not wait until it is too late.

Even though you remove yourself from danger, a truth to cling to is that God can heal and restore—however that comes about in your situation.

What escape plan for safety will you—at this moment—put together?

Week 52 Reflections

Day 1   This week's verse in full, or a portion thereof:

____

____

____

Day 2   This verse empowers me to:

____

____

____

Day 3   My response to the entreaty at the end of the message:

____

____

____

Day 4   What I most appreciate about my husband this day/week:

____

____

____

Day 5   Prayer:

____

____

____

About the Author

Mary Stone, a follower of Christ and lover of God's Word, is devoted to sharing the wisdom and encouragement she has gleaned over the many years she has studied the Bible and worked in the field of Counseling. Her mission is threefold: for God to get the glory, for readers to get victory, and for Satan to be defeated.

Mary is an inspiring keynote speaker and author, who writes with openness and sincerity. She began her career in higher education after earning a Master's Degree in Counseling at the University of Nebraska, Kearney. In 2011, Lower Columbia College in Longview, Washington conferred upon her Faculty Emeritus for her years of outstanding and dedicated service in teaching and counseling. In addition to her career as a college Counselor, Mary practiced as a Licensed Mental Health Therapist for many years.

The author's first published non-fiction book, *Run in the Path of Peace—the Secret of Being Content No Matter What*, continues to garner her speaking engagements at women's conferences, book groups, and virtual conversations.

Mary loves to write, garden, travel, do puzzles, and spend time with her family—not necessarily in that order, depending on the day and on the Pacific Northwest weather.

She and her husband make their home in Washington state.

Mary invites you to contact her at:

maryellenstone@hotmail.com and/or subscribe to her monthly devotional blog, *Sowing Seeds*, at:

https://marystonewriter.com